RHYTHMS OF
LIVING WATER

Copyright © 2021 Munday Martin

Rhythms Of Living Water: *Space Poetry*

All rights reserved. No part of this book may be used or reproduced by any means, graphic, electronic, mechanical, including photocopying, recording, taping, or by any information storage retrieval system without the written permission of the author except in the case of brief quotations embodied in critical articles and reviews.

ISBN: 978-1-955546-09-6

A Publication of Tall Pine Books
  tallpinebooks.com

*Published in the United States of America

RHYTHMS OF LIVING WATER

SPACE POETRY BY MUNDAY MARTIN

CONTENTS

nazareth above 1
crescent smile 2
none but jesus 3
my life story 4
which is why 5
jennifer 6
mom of moms 7
swirls 8
inside family jokes 10
stationery pets 11
unity of brothers 12
in a lake called galilee 14
communion 16
and honestly 18
jesus wept 19
shadows dwell where colors hide 20
one two three and plunge 21
when the labor ceases 22
hate 23
the pale face of love 24
the jesus movement 25
oh, the corporate anointing takes me to a place! 27
learn 29
pizza dreams 30
oh jerusalem 33
the girl with the long wavy hair 35
harbor 36
in case 38
the blanket 39
october 41
michigan man 42
first cry 43
south africa 44
she does 45

the blood	46
the opposite of catastrophe.	47
tinker toys	49
pretty much the last time i'll say pretty much	50
soak me up in my violent freedom praise	51
to the ONE who has always been	54
hug	55
college dreams	57
the american dream	60
inside family jokes	62
paris can't have me	63
quote	64
these teachers	65
the last beat poet	66
"reactionary"	67
the prayer meeting	68
prayer then	69
unrepented	70
african princess	71
nonsense	72
can it be that surreptitious?	73
preferably rock candy	74
tones of home	75
jbv to jbm	76
can i have this dance?	77
about munday	81

NAZARETH ABOVE

trace back millenniums, and you'll find a lion cub staring
at these same mountains

same wind
the pines and palms
furrows dying for seeds
the white, rocky, rugged, sloping precipices

a piece of land of promise
pieces
     together
          perceptions

lowly nazareth

a humble king raised in these hills
who soon the Messiah would be

but a son of a carpenter?
they'd mockingly chant
does these signs and wonders we see?

lowly nazareth
condescended by pious ones

yet situated so high and free
upon the tops of promised land's rocks

the Savior mastered carpentry

we know off to jerusalem he did die
and the story still is told

that our Nazarene King still builds us the redeemed
mansions on streets of gold

*This poem was written in Israel in Migdal HaEmek while gazing at
Nazareth situated in the mountains as I gleamed with joy considering the
humility of our Savior Jesus Christ who died for our sins.*

CRESCENT SMILE

your eye makes a crescent
in a beautiful jewish way
me?

i'm living in black-and-white photograph scrapbooks with
a smile
that looks middle eastern like yours

you make me feel successful
absent of a doctorate
yet majoring in your wild grin
flunking doubt

because consider this
did you dip your ladle in life's hope and find no reason to
believe?
not when you smiled at me that way!

way into some
supernatural joy frenzy
that sent us whirling
among a thousand manifested
     nouns
        that
          mean
           the
            same
              thing
                as
                  trust

NONE BUT JESUS

absent of the eyes of grace
entranced of you (my darling Savior)
i'd fail bereaved
of all i was

no name could bear
no wince console
the vision of my non-worth

intrinsic of no "nameness"
ever to summon emptiness

no poem, no fill,
not even void,
nothing

each hope dispelled
i'd ever gravel all holiness

until the nothing i became
fueled the consumption
of the no, i'm not

but should these eyes
see none the blood
all acceptance hails

nonetheless, i would
ever near undying love
uttering no worthy word
but Jesus

MY LIFE STORY

once upon a time
in the land of…

the end

james 4:14

WHICH IS WHY

all my fears disintegrate like judgment day
just by asking
all my lusts thrown out and cast into the flame
brimstone honey
pure unadulterated fire hell and brimstone
goodbye

their aromas burning
send our nostrils to a brilliant sigh
both you and i are seeing this change

tamed now

not unruly
in disarray
when i walked the wild pastures
of a doom, deceptive
incandescent lie life
the serpent appeared
as an angel of light

but i've read the end of the book
which is why i dance
in what were once somber corners
once cold archways
frowning
seep

today a vast open sky
on your canvas
with strong beauty and end

turned tides brought
guiltless subtleties
and keep piling above
my highest perception
all the while
you know the open end

JENNIFER

walking through that door
no man could close
unfurled by the King

was a lamb waiting by a shepherd staff
on belmont steps that spring

whose gorgeous eyes
bursting with hopeful summer
surprised me in my fall

i lost my speech
at one hot glance
my name
hard to recall

turn around now, sonnet
see the one your words cannot describe

turn around now, song
and see the one
no melody could mesmerize

like the chorus
who fell into my arms
that summer
in a daze

turn around now, beauty, and see the one which best
sums up your face

her name?

turn around now, boldness
because
she heisted your fame
and stirred your words

into a million rhythms
of ceaseless love
to the one named
jennifer

MOM OF MOMS

some say when men seek
for the love of their dreams
their quest will begin with no other

than to seek the traits and qualities
that remind them of their mother

these dreams of late
manifested delights

have become one of virtue which shines
such strength and kindness emit from the one

who i with great joy
call my bride

now, if this is true
then i no doubt have seen
there's a sparkle that sometimes
in jen's eye that gleams
and this trait that i've seen
that is sweeter than splenda
reminds me of beauty
that goes by the name linda

i love you, my one and only up bringer
that carries the feminine, motherly gender

no doubt i one day will have sons who do seek
this treasure in women much like that inside thee

SWIRLS

my head swirls
outside four walls
drenched in ecstasy

His nearness numbs
humiliation's embrace

i somehow stand
nursing with this stupid pasted smile
scarcely holding
my jesus is coming sign

well!
you try smiling
when your jaws
pine to gape

or your eyebrows
droop to discover age lines

he yanks sicknesses
out of the walking dead
ding a ling He made me sing

the megaphone speaker
tko'd the school intercom

like cats thrown at finney
wesley pummeled by pebbles
hogan riding his cycle in the sky

poor souls, i forgive
curse me out their window
in their drive-by buzzing
like a swarm of murder hornets

it was worth it that i showed up!
it was worth every microwave dinner
i threw down to make the 3:30 bell

He finds the penitent heart among my quest for the disenfranchised

His nudge is incessant
His olive press massages out
my knots of complacency

boring is the life otherwise

A poem written about my consistent preaching of the good news to my local high school on the sidewalk. Such Holy Spirit Glory! Lives changed!

INSIDE FAMILY JOKES

hi, my name is munday
why are you?

curly quasar
brought noqnoose
over today
egg…
zactly!!!

see ya soon
rocket man
ffffffffffffflower

gober
bubba

what is happening?

STATIONERY PETS

dad
can i please borrow the scissors

pencils

missy
kitty
pumpkin
brandy
jupiter
oreo

pets i'll see in heaven

and don't forget little e guy
bella and wesley

paper clip
ok bye

UNITY OF BROTHERS

spinning life
time stops
no time didn't stop
it kept going!

we just weren't in it
man, it's a euphoric carousel!
a parade of unfamiliar sentiments suddenly intersects the crossings
of our emotions drive and highway joy world

sean, charlie, caleb, jen, and i
peace, patience, do da diddy, and who cares about credit cards
and this world's chitty bang

our simplifications of childlike
curious vibes encompass us
as we swallow Emanuel's river
overflowing in our cups of perpetual desperation
syndrome

there's a light that breaches
in a million streams
for all who seek to be free
and in untrained movements
we dance into the circle
of these friendships of unity

as we laugh
the ancient sword of zion
slices through our atmosphere
of world life

and he dumps heaven's bliss
out of the envelope of His heart
into our fast car

as life liquefies into the very reason
we truly live

oh, love!

love, you're an unfathomable expansion of the heart
whose borders stretch further
than we allow into an infinite reality of pause

i will never find the words
you are a universe within
continually reaching
continually breaching

and unity makes you fly
makes you fly
makes you God
the Father, Son, and Spirit kind

and when our jars of clay burst one day
let our spirits cradle the timelessness
of Your reactor machine
which revs up the millions of streams

and the reasons we live
one revved so right
over and over
and over and over
again

IN A LAKE CALLED GALILEE

in a valley where once dwelt darkness great
there arose a brilliant light on thee
and the people wondered
as He'd often go yonder
could this Man the Messiah be?

and on a mountain high yonder
He would often go
to talk with his Dad, who loved Him so

here prayed alone the Son of God
by a lake called galilee

in a valley, where once dwelt darkness great
dwelt a man whose terror would find good fate
their name was legion for many they were
that shrilled inside his scream

Jesus, son of the most high God, what have we to do with thee?

and this carpenter's child
loved this wounded man while
by God's power
he caused them to flee

an entire pigpen dove straight to their end
in a lake called galilee

in a valley, where once dwelt darkness great
went thousands to hear what words he spake
rumors of his miracles were heard throughout
the coasts of this small sea's devout

and many a pilgrim came that day
many a pilgrim down and out

so many traveled with no bread
and compassions waters were what fed
empty stomachs of those

who would come to know
He was the Bread of Life
who loved them so

which would be broken soon for sin eternally
this humble Man was the King of Kings

and thousands of lost sheep
on the mountains believed
by a lake called galilee

Written in Peoria Galilee, Israel, in a guest house overlooking the beautiful Sea of Galilee

COMMUNION

the silent symphony
thwarts my stale plans
and fills this void with life juice
for a brand-new dawn
and so, i sing
and eat your delicacies
set before me
in your presence, there is life

i'd rather be nowhere else
just postured for praise
as i violently gaze into your beauty
in these still moments
the real kingdom swallows me
and in fidelity, i breathe

a living fire captures me
and engulfs me
kind of feels like
paradise!

kind of feels like home

i suddenly realize
as i hope to find two pair of eyes
in this quest for intimacy
all the corners of my heart expand
and run to you
like a hard field event
contest for first prize

let me see heaven for 1 millisecond
and i know i'll be on a permanent vacation
from this temporal nightmare

every beautiful song in the world
suddenly becomes envious
as you step onto the scene

every essence of man's glory

that has been captured in timeless artform suddenly forms
into one alert soul
bowing before your prevalent
imperial light

and i gasp!
and i cling to you!
and my soul loves you!
and can you come down here and
quench me?

this longing is a serene high tower
over waters
in which i would dare to plummet
in hopes that you'll catch me in your sovereignty

the whole earth is filled with your praise! and i scream
into the boundless black night
quench me!
quench me!

AND HONESTLY

along the open road
i tweak in a trance of grace
and the sunlight recalls
the fierce open ending to my desires
pliable like a lucid dream
a swift end of the monotony
of time locked days
and I find you

synchronization
study
a quick turn
a certain cluster of vibrating light particles agree to invade
earthbound kingdoms

awakening realities
starlits in hollywood
coffee shop addicts
ceos
snowboard champions
to a new trance of grace
shifting paradigms
a blazing face

a new american
trance of grace

JESUS WEPT

how the dearest citadel
mistakenly grieves the sons of men
reaching forth in peace, so to speak
yet snatching them by the hand

so soon, the warning from their lips
claims hell to pay and death to fear
when they themselves are blinded
and revelations never near

the ones who sleep
look to these
of God's men who still fail
and these of God's men
through Christ's wrists
still drive another nail

His spirit grieves
and moans for those
to walk with Him
to their eternal home

yet their churches keep on growing, collecting money on
the phone

so quick to grow within themselves
forgetting those who have no home
forgetting those who moan

naked and nothing, they alone
were Jesus Christ in woe

A convicting message to modern-day Pharisees whose
leaven I have also had to repent.
Obey the words of Christ and be free in Jesus' name!

SHADOWS DWELL WHERE COLORS HIDE

the shadows of the romancers'
bounced off the serene meadows
performing a swan dive
off the lakeside docks

munday and jennifer
however, were still there
their shadows dwelt where colors hide
as their kiss welcomed the moonrise
over lake forest

never before was there such deep embrace between them
or at least to their knowledge
the potential of their love multiplied

relentlessly in desperate equations of desire times desire times desire
equals unfeigned appetite
all the way into the 22nd century

ONE TWO THREE AND PLUNGE

oops
fell into His chasm of bliss
third time today? was yesterday friday? what's my name
munday?
monday is sunday
fine... i acquiesce
no, not reluctantly!
are you kidding me right now?

food stunk
but was good
horizons are questions

dangling on the scaffolding
of this incessant joy ride
flowers are equations
answers are nomads

starring contest with the morrow
guess who won
July 16th, 1984

traversing this quest
for His dove eyes

ask me tomorrow how He chose me, and i'll smirk and
shrug
absent of the ever-increasing answer
or nomad
or topsy-turvey
or
i could get used to this

whoopsie!
tripped into a cavern of euphoria
this is the way
of the hungry

WHEN THE LABOR CEASES

a hard week of work is best engaged
when looking back upon it on a lazy saturday

IIIlovvvee

THE PALE FACE OF LOVE

there in meekness
transcending countless insults and jeers
pain took on Man with bloody brow
ripped Son away from Father
broken heart and bitter tears
met the Man of golden love
who swallowed our cup of fears

there, in abandonment
surpassing a thousand throngs
slayed and beaten down unseen King
ripped Prince away from paradise
the chorus of death's song
met the Man of golden love
who swallowed our cup of wrongs.

To the Man who took this cup, thank You with all my life and soul!

THE JESUS MOVEMENT

mesmerization
are you alive?
then shout the rafters lose from their nails of pretty little conditions
i'm pretty fickle with systems
let's be done with traditions
their like dark cold moons rotating around obtuse dwarf planets heading for a supernova (which last i observed were pretty hesitant from withdrawing their stubborn foot from the pedal to the medal) sky fury.

in this spontaneous combustion
we all become one teeter-totter swaying away from subterfuge
preach
say that!
but don't spray that

alas
a light load (i'd say reminiscent to lillies or that paper your dog ate, remember?) on our father's shoulders suddenly manifests into a unified mantle
as we beseech the paradise place
angel flew over
dropped a bomb on me, baby
as the preacher fires his laser
boom!
whoop de doo
throw a shoe
somebody needs to run up in this presbyterian church
some boo hoo

fear goes
we go
he goes
and she goes
i reckon the dog went too
throw a shoe

in this most coveted inquisition
empty your war chess
of slaps to your neighbor's high fives
but don't fake it till you make it like
conformity beehives

revere the ancient pathway, please
ya blessed?
tell your neighbor i'm bout' to be

as small seeds sprout speedily into acres of sky reaching trees
relinquishing conceptions of the burden lifting law
who does it? who has it?
the children speak the ocean tides
the children ring the seas
branching into rivers
marshes
oceans
streams
springs
whirlpools
waterfalls
tides
roll in
roll out

as we in awe-filled ecstasy
churn our vats of faith

in this moment, we are one

the vintage pulpit street preacher breathes fire again
in this revival again

This poem was written on a love offering envelope at World Harvest Church Columbus, Ohio, witnessing the classic preaching of Rev EV Hill and later smacked down with a fresh coat of paint

OH, THE CORPORATE ANOINTING TAKES ME TO A PLACE!

the anthem

voice detector
copy houston

all through the stiff air
of this mild terrain
subject to the announcements

faded ecstasies
you knew softly
bathed away

the body of Christ
close to you
are all purposely stale
waiting for His masterpiece
in church tonight

to give them one more reason
to lose their mind

delusions of grandeur
melt their expectations
into a sea of snot

and they realized
it was the people dancing close by
that made them so severely high

the worship took us there!

we tripped on a tradition
when we were in sparkle land

we fidgeted a curl
got a breath mint out of our purse

sometimes throw out the program
and let Him be God

adjust the preamble
the anthem

LEARN

learn me life
learn me love
oh, Spirit dove

oceans' calm
breezes

the vine delights
remote
access
heaven

intravenous
liquid light dome

incessant is this my
refuge

PIZZA DREAMS

one fourth of these dreams has me finishing my
crossword puzzles
and blowing out the candlelight
to read Your word
timeless
till i fall asleep

an eighth of these dreams
has me running up my credit card
and giving the room a look around
for something unusual
another night
borrowing
and surfacing
till i fall asleep

a twelfth of these dreams
creates for me mind expansions today that will be the key
to tomorrow's survival
offering solutions
and filling the void
till i fall asleep

a sixteenth of these dreams
has me praying
and confronting doubt
during meditations
that will change my life forever
grinding and tightening
till i fall asleep

a twentieth of these dreams
has me with these sentiments
trying to relieve mentalities
years before
when i seemed more sure
desperate attempts
and finally quenched
till i fall asleep

a twenty-fourth of these dreams
has me drop kicking uncleanliness
thoughts swell up to adam bombs
and i sweat
writing fiercely
one soul
one mind
till i fall asleep

a twenty-eighth of these dreams
has me staring at the waning moon
patterns of rotation
are wearing me out
nature is far better
and i throw my television
out my window
and watch it fly to hell
i can hear it
screaming and lying
till i fall asleep

a thirtieth of these dreams
has me accidentally lured
into bubblegum pop-rock on the waves
disco in the kitchen
anti-try to behave
sporadic and thundering fads
going down a whirlpool of nothing
till i fall asleep

a thirty-sixth of these dreams
has me getting my act together
anti-throwing the towel in
figure 8
docile grouping of sane notions
to keep my composure
not stale
eloquent and hotter than angry mail
till i fall asleep

a fortieth of these dreams
has me conceptualizing numbers

(ha! as if you didn't notice by now lol)
and patterns
as i strive to flush the fear of going unnoticed in this world
opening the show
and at last encore

till they fall asleep
till they fall asleep

OH JERUSALEM

left the cool suite
under sky's canopy
in the warmth of a hostel
high in jerusalem's hills

went downstairs and gazed on promise streets
where hundreds of promises walk to the beat
of answered prayers and prophecies
yet need a friend
a smile
a hand
oh, people of jerusalem

so many have come from lands so far
one from a city and two from a clan
may i grab hold of your garments and ever chant
come my little chicks into the wings of the hen

i have heard that God is your friend

lift up your heart oh man, with no home
who sits at our marketplace waiting for change

on the highways and hedges
your quiet voice asking
penetrates compassion's clouds of rain
some ignore your plea, some stop, and some reach
but not as far as your sadness has breached

please take my bread
my water
anything
from my comfort filled life of luxuries
may i grab hold of your garments and ever sing

come my little chick into the wings of the hen
i have heard that God will mend

at last, i speak to nations and hopefully plead
to your peoples and governments

princes and kings
the Maker of heaven and earth does not sleep

and watches over israel continually
may you grab hold of their garment
and comprehend
there sits his little land in the wings of the hen
i have heard that God will defend.

For the people of Israel, I will always stand with you.

"Pray for the peace of Jerusalem they will prosper the love thee." Psalms 122:6

"Thus saith the Lord of hosts: 'In those days it shall come to pass that ten men out of all the languages of the nations shall take hold, even shall take hold of the skirt of him that is a Jew, saying, "We will go with you, for we have heard that God is with you." Zachariah 8:23

THE GIRL WITH THE LONG WAVY HAIR

beautiful smile that lights my world
the girl with the long wavy hair

strummed my guitar
furious interruption
then a voice i met that paired

this beatnik's search for a faithful friend
to a life that we could share
called her name out like a wild troubadour
the girl with the long wavy hair

must admit my stride's been spontaneous
over the years, you've corralled my heart
with the sweetest, firmest, loyal love
only heaven could impart

pray to heaven all will find a spouse
that meets your soul so fair
fall in love again and again and again
the girl with the long wavy hair

i've failed to tell you often enough
how your courage and strength can't compare
to all the wives in the world
you stand out like a pearl
and our kids are a genuine pair

no greater love has a woman than this than she lay down
her life for her friend
this you've done like breathing in air

i'm a firing my guns of poetic songs this morn'
to the girl with the long wavy hair

HARBOR

gorgeous fierce storms of ambers
alighted and enveloped your pupils surrounded by
haunting green seas
your eyes and a smile invite me
to a nuance

the list checked
the books unfurled
start
still in writing

we sail this intrepid journey
knowing well the seas call for tranquility
and i'm headed
for the harbor

there we, in unchained embrace
find new meaning to friendship
i was stranded yet for a time
hours were desperate
looking behind
when trials braided a strand
to whip us backward
the violence of loyalty
catapulted us
into harbor

we knew too well
untainted affection
angels hurriedly banded
in our direction

with your ringed hand in mine
lying down on our backs
to sail the coasts divine

the books unfurled
still in writing

we sail this intrepid excursion

knowing well the seas call for tranquility, and we're headed
for the harbor

eyes that meet a selfless heart
vibrated a symphony
intricately placed
in a world that begs for faithful friendship

when i stare into them
i fall into the ship
countless of times
inspired lesions of poems
without room for lines
about my journey
to the harbor

IN CASE

in case
i don't see you
next year

die happy

THE BLANKET

last night i had a dream
the oddest of all thoughts
ocean dwelling dragons
roamed mad seas
and atop were rumming hooves
and swirling paddles
that drove cattle powered cargo fairies through a violent spinning storm
these were pictures upon my blanket
that covered me in my sleep

last night i had a dream
the oddest of all thoughts
the ocean waters had turned to red
and out of a blood-stained sea
came a dragon's head
and to my rescue, to my surprise
came bottlenose dolphins
from the lower tides
and so, we rode the bow wave
of the cargo fairies stride

last night i had a dream
the oddest of all thoughts
the vigilant eyes of a scorpion fish
had detected us below
it came at that to ask us mad
where it was that we should go
we beseech you will be very terse
we're sorry that we cross your turf
but we're looking for what i call my home it's to my bed i go
and so, he let us cross

last night i had a dream
the oddest of all thoughts
the dragons re-emerged
and this time not distraught
i shouted out in Jesus name
be gone with you and flee

alas, drown in your lies
and cease to torment kids like me
the ocean dwelling dragons
then shrilled their final screams

last night i had a dream
the oddest of all thoughts
my dolphin caravan
had finally reached a halt
i stepped aside and a bid farewell
and a little warped it seemed

that i'd awakened
from my night's fantasy
under the blanket
of my dreams

A poem that I wrote in my history class as a sophomore in high school at the age of 16. This one thankfully was memorized which originally was written in a book of poems I lost when I was young. I added the paragraph about my authority in Jesus to bring swift victory to the dragon enemies in which I wrote about. Today I am thankful of the authority Jesus gives us as obedient believers in His blood. Amen!

OCTOBER

precious sentiments
begin to permeate my walk
decomposed smells of woods
relaying the fast summer that fled
runny noses sniffing in the free air

the sunset like a golden fire
came to court the night
look to musical horizon
of sun yawning for a nap
looks like heaven
came to kiss the earth
as we wetted lips that chapped

pounding passion for the days to come
of cool twilight months
dances fancifully in my expectations
as the stars bow to the sky

of our world of
approaching holidays
and spice tea
and pumpkin pie

that's october

MICHIGAN MAN

that was the day i deemed it was true
i could paint his face on a hot air balloon
you ain't met a finer chap
if down your lifelong path

if you haven't met
a countryside michigan man
it's behooving to do just that

mr. hawes is a chief of laughter
with a childlike heart
i wish i could impart
the joy he's brought me
then i'd sell it for free
and chivalry and honor thereafter

the outskirts of michigan
breeds such a man
and i still have failed to know how

if you haven't met
a countryside michigan man

it's behooving to do so now

FIRST CRY

hello my son
i curiously say
as i ponder in intense streams
that flow from a river of deepest love
which today has flowed to me

his first cry of life
pierced the earth's atmosphere
as lesions of God's angels
hurriedly cheered
and left my heart pumping wild love itself
with pools full of joy-filled tears

hello my son
when our eyes first met
then jealous became the seas
which contain not the water
to quench this love
we now share eternally

hello my son

To my blessed firstborn son, Samuel Munday Martin, who invaded my life with unknown love on 10-03-06. Welcome to our world, son. I love you, Dad

SOUTH AFRICA

quiet nights
in elephant inhabited land
groans evaporate in my ears
no light pollution
in the star lit south african
countryside sky
trees speak
creeks tainted
with unfamiliar smell
black cascade
sphere horizon
then dawn
undressed feelings
fancifully spawned

SHE DOES

she does softly
in a strange caravel
in a no man's land

and to alleviate
she does drift
into another perspective
grabs daydreams
or illusions from her kitty cat bag
as her soul radiates
all the way into the
21st-century

THE BLOOD

walk the sea to Him
drown
  drown

eden missed with fury
fail
  fail

left the lamb to die
tear
  tear

rip the temple veil
drip
  drip

death in devastation
fly
  fly

promised a return
wait
  wait

we wait for heaven's sake
time
  time

spoke in tongues so drunk
flame
  flame

the world turned upside down
quake
  quake

quiet desperation
wait
  wait

jesus come again
fate
  fate

THE OPPOSITE OF CATASTROPHE

everywhere sometimes
mystery gatherings
court the night
i park by venus and the lake

to absorb this immutable date
remember i was slovenly dressed

the world, however, does not wait
as hungry horizon devours the sun
just in time for mars to figure skate
the infinity symbol
on my lack of new jokes

the saints walk up west end
praying for our city
at the lake, you wistfully grip my hand

egos like dewey eyes swell up
protuberant but careless enough
to fall deeply in love
and abort the past
which ran like a wild stallion
into mercury

reminiscent of swallowing
our vitamins in time
to bolt out the side door
in a rampage for the day
prior to sunset

the moon reflects on your eyes
like refrigerator magnets
you were in the silent wind throughout

that's why i vehemently
toast to the morning star
and then i'm like flying
you are you , i am i
this mystery
indelibly courts the night

TINKER TOYS

waiting, tinker toys, careers
the wait
has it been hours?
millenniums?

you know, a one world currency
isn't too far from becoming a reality
yakety smack

we put up our stockings
well
this past Christmas
they were handed out
our own one

but time didn't stop
to re-gather itself
it's a complex wheel we tried to label

playing trivial pursuit
won't help solve it

you're gonna need a vacuum
preferably a black hole
that sucks up all matter
then you can examine
where it goes
or intertwines

ask for one next Christmas
time will have, however, beat you there

PRETTY MUCH THE LAST TIME I'LL SAY PRETTY MUCH

11:56
done with lunch
want holiness
cherubs rest
backpack people stride by
some real turbulent
but sublunary
which means under the moon
hence mortal and subject
to change

12:14
internal ache
confidence swelling
external obedience
sometimes suffer
deep stain of lamb's blood
warms the air
of the rooms
of this cold world's
hopelessness
sleep

awake and stealthy
a mist of breath
breathes upon
my mirror
and writes the word
happiness
no, wait!
holiness

SOAK ME UP IN MY VIOLENT FREEDOM PRAISE

i mean it's tangible presence
have you felt it?
i will instigate
reflect, search out, jump in
relax, roll
presence soak
ah!
presence soak

forget the limitations
reach out
dive in
incessant seek
saturate my body
the veils getting thin

God

some publishers
are ashamed of that name

God

what ignorance
have you felt this thick
rich life dance
free beyond the
meaning of the word ecstasy

that's exactly my point
what is this love?
i'm ruined
i'm undone
i'm high
i'm plugged

therapeutic instant
electric vibrations
angelic voices
resonating vibrations

in this realm
tears pour out for nations
i can feel it
can you feel it?
it's drawing us up
we're going up
our prayers are reaching
beyond the boundaries
of stupid wussy doubt

i will soak this time
i'll drink the river
i will laugh
i will gaze up to the
streets made of gold
and I will laugh at vain religion

fierce winds blowing
i will defy the strongholds
barely a minute
and the good news winds
have blown every
misconception away
for those who don't know
it's Jesus day

that's it
that's the freedom
i have so longed for

as i dance
the faces of tradition
gaze mockingly at my free soul
as i become more vile
in my violent freedom praise
cry out
dance like the thunder

freedom praise

when the move is on
there's no time to behave
breaking down the city dam
just in time for sunset haze

scream one more time
say goodbye to the chains!

TO THE ONE WHO HAS ALWAYS BEEN

slow chambers moving amidst
Your time ticking
tectonics of love unending
touching the reaches of fading seas
conjuring unplaced silence

from stable ice glaciers
to fields of wheat
earth
sends it's a lullaby frequencies
to a chain of sun glowing birchwood trees
too late, these folding mysteries
do not fulfill my list of yearnings

still, somehow you stabilize
my every ambition
as i sing a song of this blissful twilight

tokens of expression
release my soul
to a lofty mesmerizing view
where a songbird mocks a time-filled universe
from a willful heart and defiant perch
while i bless this universe in ardent fierceness

while opinions gather
together and implode
while all creation spirals like
an infinite galaxy
around the One who has always been

daring is this
romance

HUG

an embrace so deep
the world could not see
caught us both by surprise
enamored songs filled space and time
it was almost like a dance
a hug good night turned into chance
never felt that deep
felt like healing
felt like i knew you somewhere
some time

you were reeling me in
for a spin delight
felt like morning kissed the night
felt like desert kissed the rain
felt like mystery unchained

i was gorgeous in your eyes
i swept you off your feet
that night on 16th St.
kicked my friend under the table
in our taco first date treat

it was then i really knew
my heart had clearance for takeoff
it's the hug we often spake of
that lit a fire
before summer came
we were two kids
healing from shame

He created us to fit together
in that embrace
the night i forgot my name

it was you from all those years
the answer to all my tears
alleviated on that eve
where forever we were pleased

to take the key to our past
and throw it away
we would never be the same

the hug that took us by surprise
may
june
july
and every day that passes by

COLLEGE DREAMS

sarah, moon, patrick, and me
we drifted by cummings tonight
i fingered the piano
the measure of the routine is family
says the notion
"we are still so young
we have our lives."
screams the notion
"let's have plenty,"
deranged competence
at its best

do i need a house with bills
to be content?
security is the roof and food
no, i want to be wealthy
but generous

sarah is a big joy fun
obedient to her violence
for the kingdom

busy numbers follow our footsteps
on this campus
like a network of high schoolers
who still don't get it
no, i want to be famous
but generous
to make Him famous

i keep walking with suction cup feet
on this landscape of my indecisiveness
fine!
joy is my major
hope is my minor

moon is a sea of tears
attracted to light
with a hint of sunshine
to finish the long list of ingredients

that helps you see her walls

patrick
give him another name
the food stunk but good
triceratops was always
getting picked on by that rex

sometimes when i cross
jocks on my walk
i jump in my manhole
and my feet get tight
i can manage
the faces of difference
and rex

we are young
we have our lives
we have indifference
yeah, the beat is played all over town

our feet on these streets
they're like massive smokestacks
you dig?

puffing out humor
that bleaches boredom
hello invisible angels

loyalty is great
if you know "un-back-stabbers"
make it sound good

well, we will whine when we worry
why would we want wonders
whenever we walk

miracles are fun
friends like us skip the politics
skip the lunacy
so, it's 1999 already
and my honesty can be barbecued

see you in the next century
or wake up and smell the noise
so thick you could floss your teeth with it

it's called find a career
me?

it will find me
oh, those holidays
oh, those crusades
optimism rivers
dream a dream inside of a dream
frequency
audio
tweak

sarah, moon, patrick, and me
we drifted by curlew tonight
with the same stealth of cop cars
like busy bees
intrigued by notions
of he, me, and she

THE AMERICAN DREAM

yada yada yada
something way too underrated
too much money love cradling
your nerves
paintings all about
driveway steaming with the company car
and a murderous billfold
tucked away for a rainy day

maybe to renovate
the whitewashed tombs
you've become
busy circumstances
that will continue to make you toil
through retirement
then a spinning landscape

next?
an ostentatious fly away
down the wrong highway
psycho youth today
tomorrow?
the great american dream

and the cherry on top
more pill love
because they never truly
trusted Him
they ran to the conformity barn
and willingly calmed their nerves
and stayed in darkness
long enough to be immune
to the light

and swallowed their
money crave syndrome
placing the placid numbness
in their portfolios
their fellow man

last in their plans
then a fancy funeral

never underestimate this
silent growing hate

INSIDE FAMILY JOKES

and
chittlefootderye
hasha shee fy ya dad bum
constantinople
ya bunch of…
happy thoughts

PARIS CAN'T HAVE ME

love
some accordions
and then some
gaudy dinner
and lastly
some repulsive
stinky cheese
that's paris

QUOTE

there's woman
there is man
one is
two are
what is the splanchna...Greek?
that's right!
for innermost being

well, why does the groan start there
don't say it oozes cause it gushes
don't say it's heavy
it can be easy streams
if you yield to Holy Spirit
it's a well
it's the very beauty I strive for
usually on the floor
ha!

from your innermost being, it flows
picture your soul weeping
laughing with joy
then you framed it and pasted
it's a well

why does the groan start there?
it doesn't have to be sadness

don't say it's love
because it's the lack of it
don't say love hurts
love heals
unforgiveness hurts
the real monster is the bitterness
the real pain is the state of a hard heart

don't say it's incompatibility
it's misunderstanding
and don't say it
don't say it
don't say love hurts
it's the lack of it

THESE TEACHERS

teachers
did you feel the essence of His presence? perhaps
dismayed
maybe discreet
because for now
the undertow of lies
carries these fearless teachers
none return
not one

forever is not a cycle
it will always be
meaning never is never
future is forever
forever is a place
the sea of time glistens and fades
the world, however, does not wait

these teachers come in many shapes
mind swelling
lasso sweeps
try to stand
can't in the end
moonlit silvery eyes
staring into the cosmos
and yet they still doubt
turning to ellipses
and branching into open streams
further than the wise can see

can you deem what this world is for?
teachers can you sense
the essence of His presence?
how reclamations proved leery
like pangaea
and they all tried to believe
as scientists perform a mortal debate
the world, however, does not wait
get saved

THE LAST BEAT POET

boom tap
boom boom boom
tap

no is to not
but not to never
yes, is to be
but not forever

no, let no reign safe in bliss
yes, this will agree to no
hence this yes is understood
as being
uh-huh
temporary yes

no, this is not uh-uh
till the end of the story
with a yes
with a run-on sentence

no, and yes
which will rule free will
not to be
which will rule consequence
never to forever
which will rule eternity

disclude the never
and say yes to be forever
but use the no to disclude
the not

and put a yes
in the empty spot
yes
uh-huh
yes

the empty spot...

"REACTIONARY"

and this excavation of time
and sojourning here in
temporal fascination
runs like three streams
emerging into three energies of prayer

and now?
and now what?

THE PRAYER MEETING

deep wise honest glow
saturated with aged love
in that man's nuanced smile
pat your back jack
grin attack

international lifetime
spread across
wrinkles with no boundaries
tearing up with
compassion's red waters
lead
lead

challenges of memorizing
promises of prophecies
by a noble chief
follow
lead

hebrew blessing spoken
over two longing travelers
lit to blaze the trails
we curiously journeyed on
as we slept in airports
with daring synergy

dream last night
still burning inside
like glowing lightning
ever seen sheet lighting?
kind of like that
but rainbow flashes
and yet subtle

mercy Lord that's all i ask
and great God please understand
i'll keep traveling down this heritage road
till them plow handles bust in my hand

(A poem written about a meeting with Don Finto who encouraged our missions to Israel, ending with a nod to my grandfather Riley Munday's poem he wrote titled "Plow handles"

PRAYER THEN

and in the tents
them sunbeams
pierce through
on a delivered soul
with 26-year-old hands
brushing through their rays

a mind that teleports
to familiar sentiments
gathering inspirations
from his painted youth

that's still me
the smell of vinyl boat seats drying
from salty mist
that spewed out
of the long island sound
driving 25 mph
and "ice cream and candy
all in one"

actually, they chanted
that twice
on a home video of us
water skiing lake ouachita
it was the fat frog ice cream pop commercial
remember?

slip me through life's narrow door
looking back
mortality
pain
fear
hopelessness

fades
fades
turn around?
lights forever rays

UNREPENTED

who lets themselves
ever abide in obsessions
absent of discretions
and when quenching their wants
then
release their confessions

having not done so first
live in incessant oppression

who?
fearful this is
let this be a lesson

AFRICAN PRINCESS

black sandals and olive-green skirt
that meets white sweater of
kaleidoscope dreams

african princess sits before me
she's a little light under blue skies

she stares virtuously into the horizon
and she's happy in her poverty
she dances on down a dusty road
as she waves her arms frantically

praising her Maker
in a tribal sway

and the angels that see her Father's face shed tears over
her beaming brown
the tears make her face shine
in extraordinary ways

she's happy in her poverty
but I know one day
she'll be an african queen

praising her Maker
in a tribal sway sway

Written about a small child who caught me off guard with
joy in her great poverty while I was on a mission trip in
Kampala Uganda

NONSENSE

you have such an excellently toned
spirit about you
did you know britain has these
strange highlands
where people claim fortune
to some lowly
umm...
half cent pastrey eating
street walkers that streamed
through the 18th century
and stopped at the 1967 portal
just in time to turn off
the frozen water spicket
for an october night
of surprises?

CAN IT BE THAT SURREPTITIOUS?

america
like there's nothing behind your beauty
like life is all escape
honey find it
severe
reach above the pied piper
monotony that rings on each street
severe
why can't you see
be good
don't flea
like your stiff with fear
honey find it
like sterilized
or rather innocualted
groups of thoughts
maddening
honey reach
severe
like clouds collapse and rain
honey breathe
refrain

PREFERABLY ROCK CANDY

the volcano of emeralds erupts
location comes over and says
"my a dainty spectacle
of bloody joy"

direction sings
"go there
get whimsical
go inside, pray tell
i do say ole' chap"

coalition is making me not want to try
why direction
to what demise is this directed
holes
numbers
pieces
fragments
electricity
nothing inland

everything is blowing
through a tube
of tubes
of tubes
of speculation

TONES OF HOME

placed here in my father's land
a saint to be
the matadors in my head scarcely survive with their pride
their red
guess what
the time is now
affiliation with such concepts
is far from making me scared
God makes me ready like quickly

these tones of home are like harmless asteroids
causing fire in the sky
dispersing grains of sand

and to my dear mother that lives to serve
every memory of her is like no words
can't express this mere gratitude
it makes me fervently listen to every sweet
vibration she leaves behind
of her humility and the essence of my beatness
calm

like tones of home in my father's land
hanging around here again

JBV TO JBM

and these myriads of deep sentiments
you send to me
send me to the Son I seek
i sense this is the place to be
since we see, we are called together
sensibly

and when we embrace
in our oceans of holy love
the host of heaven shout amen
are you sure the scarlet reeves
beneath the sea
did not give you their prized possession?

even the eyes the gaze at me
like a twilight sky cascade
your love pounds deep
like heart relays
as we in awesome ecstasy
peer to the truth the way

oh yes, the life
it's clearer now
i will fall as deep as love permits
i could stay right here
and see your world
and search your humble spirit

and perhaps the tides
that whisper our name shiloh
will tonight roll in
as you and i roll out
around the world
in a quest for nations that we fit in

and perhaps the ones that shout shiloh
shall shout jbv to jbm

To my dear wife Jennifer
(Jennifer Beth Vincent to Jennifer Beth Martin)
a good change!

CAN I HAVE THIS DANCE?

today i dance to the blissful tune
of sailing with little you

your chinkapin eyes
wild with wonder brown
brown hair
brown everything!

full head of it was gleaming with the
florescent light reflection
of the hospital room
when you first peeled out of the womb

like a revved-up machine
going to saturn
you were already on your way
you little energy machine

oh yeah
back to that dance
the one that tears up my
wondering soul

christopher cross
and pink flamingos
light our little night
from the tv
with a symphony
no other 80s song could
fly

again again
you hurriedly proclaimed
and we'd dance again
and we'd dance again
did i mention we danced again?

as i carried you those
summers sneezing
out pure joy world

again
again daddy
and i flipped you through the air
like an acrobat
flying like dumbo

and my, the years flew too
and my, the tears do groom

me for the day that i'll
not hold back one
and leave all to chance

yes
when prince charming
woos you off of your feet
you'll still fly through the air

and me feeling a bit like dumbo
on your wedding day
i'll subtly prance

and once more
i'll cut in for a brief ecstasy
and ask, "can i have this dance?"

to my dear JennaBeth, i love you with all my heart! daddy

ABOUT MUNDAY

MUNDAY MARTIN is a cutting-edge gospel recording singer, songwriter, poet, painter, acrobat, worship leader, and preacher. He is a solid believer that radical, creative expression of originality through the arts can ultimately glorify Jesus and cause a harvest sound in the earth to bring many to the saving knowledge of Jesus Christ.

Both Munday and his wife Jennifer are authors that preach and teach the uncompromised word of God, followed by the miraculous alongside Munday's music ministry. Munday was radically saved in 1999 shortly after encountering a dream from the Lord where he saw a glimpse of both Heaven and Hell in the middle of the night while lost in college. After this incredible encounter, Munday gave his life to Jesus and was called into an impacting global ministry to the nations with a ravishing love for His Savior. Munday is committed to making obedient disciples of Jesus Christ. He lives with his loving wife and two beautiful children in the outskirts of Nashville, Tennessee.

www.ingramcontent.com/pod-product-compliance
Lightning Source LLC
LaVergne TN
LVHW052234110526
838202LV00094B/119